MA RTHA'S VINEYARD

$\mathcal{N}$OW & $\mathcal{Z}$EN

MARTHA'S VINEYARD

Now & Zen

Communities, Traditions,
and Transformations

Susan Klein AND Alan Brigish

brigishEYE

DEDICATIONS

To my silent partner and best friend, Joyce

Without your love, constant assistance and encouragement, I could not accomplish half of what I do

——APB

To Ann Nelson,

former proprietor of Bunch of Grapes Bookstore——

for inspiring us to create this volume, and for her life-long dedication to all who love books,

and

with gratitude to all those who continue to work for the preservation of the Vineyard

——SK

ALSO BY SUSAN KLEIN:

Through A Ruby Window — A Martha's Vineyard Childhood

ALSO BY ALAN BRIGISH

The Brigish Collection 2006: Limited Edition
Eye Contact: Windows on the Soul of India
Breathing in the Buddha: A Photographic Exploration of Buddhist Life in Indochina

It's an ongoing story! For forthcoming photographs and essays by Brigish and Klein, join our free serial e-book at www.mv-zen.com

To purchase books in quantity for gifts, incentives, or corporate use, please contact Alan at (508)696-3109 or alan@brigish.com.

The introduction and chapters 2, 7, 8, 15, 16, 17, 18, 19, 20, 21, 22, 23, and 24 were previously published as e-book chapters.

FIRST EDITION, JULY 2010

Cataloging-in-Publication Data

Klein, Susan, 1951–
Martha's Vineyard : now & zen : communities, traditions, and transformations /
by Susan Klein and Alan Brigish.
p. cm.
Essays.
ISBN-13: 978-0-615-36699-9
ISBN-10: 0-615-36699-6

1. Martha's Vineyard (Mass.)—History. 2. Martha's Vineyard (Mass.)—Social life and customs.
3. Martha's Vineyard (Mass.)—Pictorial works. I. Brigish, Alan, 1942– II. Title.

F72.M5K54 2010   974.4'94
QBI10-600085

BOOK DESIGN BY JENNIFER ANN DADDIO / BOOKMARK DESIGN & MEDIA INC.

PRINTED AT SHERMAN PRINTING CO., INC. CANTON, MA
www.shermanprinting.com

Contents

Author's Preface

Ten years ago, when Della Hardman, my next-door neighbor and town columnist for the *Vineyard Gazette*, asked me what I would write about if I had the opportunity, I said, "The transmogrification of the Vineyard."

"Do it," spake she of the far-seeing eye. So I wrote an essay about creating common story by exercising common sense for the common good, and Mr. Reston, the *Gazette* editor, made it an op-ed piece.

After that, daunted, I wrote quietly for myself . . . until 2008. As I stepped out of the FedEx office one afternoon, a man popped out of a car and said, "Are you Susan Klein?" I answered in the affirmative, then asked, "Who are you?"

He said, "I'd like to run an idea by you over lunch. I'm Alan Brigish."

Changes to the Island have been the subject of essays and articles by gifted writers for more than a hundred years. I add to them my views on the complexities, celebrations, and intriguing layers of this unique community; the subjects are diverse, but not exhaustive.

My thanks to Ann Nelson for suggesting to Alan years ago the concept of such a book; to Kerry Scott for her reader's sensibility; to Susanna Sturgis for her superb editing skills; to Jen Daddio for her keen designer's eye; to English teacher Harry Dorr, who, in 1964, said, "My dear Miss Klein, you are a writer"; and to Alan Brigish, collaborator of the first order, whose stirringly beautiful photographs capture every mood of this beloved Island.

Susan Klein
April, 2010

Photographer's Note

ON WASHING ASHORE

Thirty-one years ago, I was a *guest* here.

But, I sensed it the very first time my feet touched Vineyard sand—that something in the air.

Shortly thereafter, I became a *summer visitor*—spending a week or more, almost every year.

I would feel it in line at the ferry—something just beyond my reach.

Eventually, I became a *summer resident*, often *renting* in the same neighborhood, and securing rental dates for the following year before returning to "America."

Now I would anticipate it, that certain something, compelling, extraordinary.

Year in and year out I returned, until eventually, I moved here, more or less, as circumstances allowed – that feeling in the air still beckoning.

I had become a *wash ashore*, as high as I will ever get in the order of things on this Island.

I became aware of places seldom seen, even those hiding in plain sight. The off-season, the past, the small, the private, it all educated me. Occasionally, I would catch a glimpse of something secretive, yet ubiquitous.

Now, when I travel even a short distance, that certain something holds a place within.

Through Susan's glorious prose about Zen, and my images of Now, I hope you will learn some of these secrets and take them into your heart to help protect this piece of Paradise.

There it is . . . that something in the air.

Alan Brigish
April, 2010

Island in Transition

Our island way of life, relatively unchanged for centuries, is gone. What was once accessible or limitless, bountiful or organic in nature has been altered. Those who lived it, mourn. Those who did not witness the transformation cannot be expected to understand the depth of that loss—freedoms we took for granted that exist now only in memory.

What we knew as children as our birthright—a spirited liberty—we expected to retain as adults. Most of us didn't see the change coming, the extent of its reach, or its velocity. Some were unaware, some wore blinders. Others' shouts of, *Beware!* went unheeded. Where there once was an easy balance of personal freedom and tourist trade, there has occurred a diminishment of the former in service to the latter resulting in a disturbing imbalance—the island as commodity.

When natives and long-term islanders bemoan the changes, many newcomers utter something akin to, "Well, you can't turn the clock back, *now*." When that is stated cavalierly, an islander's hackles can be raised right rapid. We are tardy in becoming acutely aware. And the signs were there. So, what now?

The truth is we've lost much—and we grieve the losses. But, that clock indeed cannot be rewound. Our current ever-changing community is teeming with extremely creative and concerned people. No matter when any of us arrived, no matter how long our ancestors have trod the island sands, no matter where we were born—if we call this place *home*—or *summer home*—our creativity must serve our concerns for preserving and conserving what remains of this stunning island and perpetuating the traditions we hold dear.

This series of essays and images addresses the lost and retained traditions of the past, acknowledges and celebrates what has been conserved and gained, and beseeches the community of the present to cultivate the future with a caring hand.

HEATH HEN
TYMPANUCHUS CUPIDO CUPIDO

THE SOLE REMAINING HEATH HEN IN THE WORLD WAS SEEN FOR THE LAST TIME NEAR THIS SPOT ON MARCH 11, 1932; THIS EASTERN RACE OF THE GREATER PRAIRIE CHICKEN WAS DECLARED EXTINCT IN 1933. DURING MATING SEASON, THE MALES MADE A LOUD "BOOMING" SOUND BY INFLATING THE ORANGE AIR SACS ON THEIR NECKS, A SOUND THAT COULD BE HEARD AS FAR AS ONE MILE AWAY. A STAPLE IN THE EARLY COLONISTS' DIET, THE HEATH HEN WAS MORE IMPORTANT THAN THE WILD TURKEY TO THE SURVIVAL OF THE PILGRIMS AT PLYMOUTH COLONY IN THE HARD WINTER OF 1620-1621. DESPITE THE PASSAGE OF VARIOUS PROTECTIVE LAWS, BY 1845 THE ONLY BIRDS LEFT WERE ON MARTHA'S VINEYARD, HAVING ONCE BEEN WIDESPREAD FROM COASTAL NEW ENGLAND SOUTH AT LEAST TO MARYLAND. IN 1908 THE COMMONWEALTH OF MASSACHUSETTS SET ASIDE 600 ACRES HERE AS A HEATH HEN RESERVATION. ADDITIONAL LAND WAS ADDED LATER UNTIL THE RESERVATION TOTALED NEARLY 5,000 ACRES, MOST OF WHICH ULTIMATELY BECAME THE MANUEL F. CORRELLUS STATE FOREST. THE HEATH HEN THRIVED ON THE RESERVATION, ITS NUMBERS RISING FROM ABOUT 50 IN 1908 TO ABOUT 2,000 IN EARLY 1916. BUT IN MAY 1916 A GREAT FIRE SWEPT THE RESERVATION, DESTROYING MANY NESTING FEMALES AND THEIR EGGS, REDUCING THE POPULATION TO ABOUT 150. PRIMARILY DUE TO INBREEDING, DISEASE AND PREDATION, DESPITE EFFORTS TO PROTECT AND PROPAGATE THE BIRD, ITS NUMBERS SLOWLY DWINDLED TO 28 IN 1923, ABOUT 30 IN 1927, AND ONLY 3 IN 1928. THE LAST BIRD, KNOWN AS "BOOMING BEN", LIVED ALONE FROM 1929 UNTIL 1932.

1

Grieving the Past

Our culture not only leaves us wanting when it comes to grieving our beloveds, but also things, practices, traditions, and events left by the wayside when "progress" invades our way of life. We're conditioned to blame and complain, but not to note the loss by ritualizing the passage of those things in a healthy way. Instead we drag around the mourned-for past or the "good old days" like a wagonload of rocks, and we're expected to be stoic and move on. It's not a wonder we limp instead of cruise into the future.

Perhaps most of us have a special spot to which we return again and again for spiritual renewal. We are creatures in love with "place." When my "own" woods were clear cut and the very undulation of the earth was bulldozed away, I was deeply saddened by the implications of what it meant to *not* be able to lie on the floor of that forest, the sun diffusing through pine branches, their heated scent bestowing a peaceful essence. The tree canopy, my very special "cathedral" which I had relied on since I was four years old to help glue me back together when my nerve endings got frayed, had been reduced to flattened acres of yellow dirt.

Much of what we offer up as complaint about change and growth is really unresolved grief over the loss of a way of life and the absence of a cultural convention to express it; preservation is the counterpoint, and the work must be perpetuated.

2

Sublime Approval

A tradition perhaps popular on another distant island has begun here in recent years. Clapping for the sunset at Menemsha now occurs every evening of the summer, and quite frankly, it grates on the nerves of Vineyarders who practice a longstanding tradition of our own—

observing silence as a response to wonder.

First swim of the season; dusk pinkletink chorus in spring; nor'easter on the Chop; beach plum jelly in January; skinny dipping in sea foam; fishing the rip; gazing at meteor showers from the beach; a mess of blue shell crabs; Gay Head Cliffs—anytime; rock-rumbling tide at Squibnocket; a lady slipper—suddenly—in a pine forest; littlenecks on the half shell; Ocean Park at dawn; sailing the Sound; return of the osprey; snow-frosted sea grass; Menemsha sunset—

the sublime requires no applause.

3

Ethereal Sense

The perception of the Vineyard as a place somewhat "other" is not new. Created in part by the procession and in part by the recession of the glacier, the Island is, in fact, an amalgamation of many places. So, of course, She is unique. In spite of seemingly unstoppable change, there remains that ethereal "sense of something beyond the tangible."

The hustle and bustle of Day masks that perception. But with the Moon's refreshment, the Island shimmers once more as the Sun peels back the Night.

4

Gritty Reality

On Island, the flash and spark of the outer world's manipulation of reality holds little importance, and in fact, meets with a measure of disdain, as Islanders eschew pretense. This has always been a place to drop the trappings of artifice, to enjoy languid and rich musings of "the great and small." To come away refreshed—and somehow new—is the Island's inherent gift.

But because we view life through a lens of authenticity, we cannot ignore the Island's peculiar attribute. Its "gritty reality" makes it at once harsh and lovely, dependable and transient, a paradise or a trap. Truth has an ample wardrobe.

Traditions continued as ever, as part of daily living in the home and in the community. The powwow had its own evolution. The Aquinnah people hosted powwows with drumming and dancing and socializing, inviting members from mainland tribes in celebration of intertribal kinship and friendship. Though the long-held tradition of the powwow lapsed in the middle of the last century, it has recently resumed at the urging of the young people of the Wampanoag tribe of Aquinnah, and is now a highly-anticipated annual event.

The Wampanoag people hold positions in all walks of life. But, as with all cultures everywhere, when it's time to celebrate, street clothes are set aside; many don stunningly beautiful regalia for this event. Though the modern powwow is a social and cultural exchange and open to *all* people, surely the vibration of the drum on the air and the dance on the earth revitalizes that which is collective and ancient.

Where sand meets clay and clay meets sky, this land is the beginning of something wondrous.

This land is the beginning.

This land.

15

Joy in the Morning

The Polar Bears who gather daily at the Inkwell hail from far and wide—their points of reference—friendship and exercise on the shore at Oak Bluffs. Innkeeper Myrtle O'Brien and her guests arranged an early morning beach schedule in the 1940s; so it began—and so it continues more than sixty years later. Individually the "bears" come from a wide range of backgrounds, but here, they are just folks enjoying the "healing waters."

The modern-day, eclectic group includes summer residents, their guests, weekenders, and a few year-rounders, as well as occasional additions the gregarious crew accumulates on a dance floor or walking by a porch, creating an ever-changing daily mix. Some folks come for a day, while others have been steadfast participants for thirty or forty years. The operative word is "Welcome" and the most frequent parting words are "I can't wait to join you (tomorrow—next summer—next time)."

The "bench bears" muse or chat or gaze out to sea. Simultaneously, there are yoga groups on the beach and joggers, walkers, parents pushing carriages, dog-walkers passing by, each greeted with a cheerful, "Good Morning!" Some "bears" exercise—women (and several men) of all ages (this summer, from 11 – 94) join the circle in the water at 7:30-ish, the elders helped and supported if need be. While they stretch their bodies, they sing. Sometimes a prayer is offered up. They chorus a daily affirmation, "I am the source of my joy and infinite possibilities."

Some "bears" swim, and though unintended, the synchronicity of their loop around the buoy holds a rhythmic beauty. This glorious collection is as much a celebration of life as it is a celebration of this place—together, a summer rose turning its face to the morning sun.

Daily announcements of the "goings-on" are delivered on the sea wall and with this interesting and interest*ed* group, there's *always* something going on. Each

Monday, the pot luck "bear breakfast" is a relaxing, delicious, and satisfyingly social commencement (and usually the largest gathering) of the week. It may be the only place to eat grits at the beach in New England! People visit for hours.

Though the Polar Bears are together only in summer and summer is short, they carry to the beach and home again a sense of inclusion and respect for others and a celebration of our differences through experiencing our far more numerous similarities—the friendships and the effects of collectively enjoying the healing waters have staying power.

What a world it would be if each of us began the day embraced by the camaraderie and acceptance of playful, yet responsible companions shouting to the sky that we are the source of our joy . . . ahhhh, infinite possibilities *indeed!*

The Vital and Vibrant 4th

As children, we anticipated the July 4th excursion to Edgartown to take in that rare and wonderful "blink-and-you-missed-it" parade to be followed by hot dogs, ice cream, and fire works. The parade back then was all about civic and national pride, flags and fire trucks, Girl Scouts, the Edgartown Boys' Club Marching Band, a convertible sporting prom queen and court in pastel confection, civic organization representatives wearing uniforms or insignias identifying their affiliations, all celebrating our nation's birthday and heralding the beginning of summer.

Participant to spectator ratios are probably about the same, though the once primarily civic parade has grown to include additional cultural entertainments, church groups, our Brazilian community, and even "floats" advertising family businesses. The sensory overload of the Mardi Gras atmosphere prevails from exuberant beginning to weary end of the three-mile route, filling our eyes with color and movement, the noise thrumming our sternums and rattling the clapboards of Edgartown's lovely homes. Babies ride shoulders, elders in rockers wave to the crowds, kids cruise on bikes and skateboards, Jabberwocky campers prance and enchant, people carry signs, bunting twines porch rails and balconies, flags snap in the wind.

The friendly mob cheers and roars its delight as friends and neighbors stroll the streets in a formless gaggle. And then, drum rolls announce our local veterans as they march by in parade dress. The heart skips a beat, and we recall the meaning of the day and the sacrifices of each generation that underscore this celebration—including those made by indigenous nations who originally occupied this great land.

Amidst the growth and change of this observance, its most striking aspect remains—the July 4th parade is the vital and vibrant embodiment of our beloved First Amendment ensuring freedom of peaceable assembly, freedom of religion, freedom of speech.

We are not a perfect nation, but on the 4th of July our thoughts rest a moment on the evolving dream that is America.

17

The Feast of the Holy Ghost

The Feast of the Holy Ghost, held here for nearly a hundred years, celebrates the generous heart of Isabela, compassionate Queen of Portugal, who, against her husband's wishes, dispensed food from the royal kitchens (and possibly jewels and money from the counting house) to the poor. When questioned about what she might be concealing under her cloak, Isabela, praying quickly and fervently, answered, "Roses!" And so it was, that when she opened her cloak at King Diniz's insistence, not bread—but roses—spilled upon the palace stones.

Saturday night at The Feast is dedicated to merrymaking. But, the Sunday celebration includes much more. Traditionally, Portuguese clubs sporting brilliant finery arrived together on the ferry with the band from New Bedford. Now only the energetic Grupo Folclorico do Clube Madeirense and the band make the journey. The men wear white, the women's striped skirts reflect the colors of the Portuguese flag.

Little girls in their First Communion dresses carrying the scepter and crown of the Queen (canonized in the 17th century) follow the Modron, who leads the long and jubilant procession, stopping at Our Lady Star of the Sea to bless the crown, and at the cemetery to remember those who have passed. At the PA, the band plays the spirited music cherished through the ages, the singers and audience join together in song, and dance the Shamarita.

While sweetbread, cooked lobsters, and commemorative articles are auctioned off to support the many acts of generosity of our PA Club, the huge crowd gleefully indulges in the sopas (pronounced "soop áge"), concocted for days from beef and vegetables and spices, and the ubiquitous and glorious linguica—free on Sunday, to emulate the generosity of the queen.

Tricia Bergeron finds joy in her position as feast leader, the Modron, "It honors my family, the Amarals, who have always contributed their time and energy and leadership to this community." The most difficult part? . . . convincing the younger generations of the importance of this tradition and the need to carry it forward. The early Azorean immigrants did not have it easy, but they've built a legacy through the PA with practices of civic benevolence in grand proportion. To see this tradition celebrating the miracle of roses wane would break our hearts.

The richness of the Portuguese traditions provide the cultural tapestry on which a good portion of the story of the Island is woven. All hail Queen Isabela and those who honor her name!

18

A Grand Night for Singing

During our childhood, on the first Wednesday morning in August, hundreds of poles were erected on the greensway surrounding the Tabernacle of the Martha's Vineyard Camp Meeting Association. Thousands of colorful furled lanterns were set beneath a grid of "clothes lines" that had been strung between the poles. That night, at the signal, dozens of Boy Scouts lit the candles set in the bases of the lanterns, which they then carefully unfolded and suspended from the lines—the result —a mid-air flickering kaleidoscope.

Everyone walked the circle and the older children ran about beneath a bobbing fairyland of lights. All was peaceful until one year in the early '70s. Due to a transportation miscalculation, lingering crowds were huge, and vandals destroyed a good deal of the beauty all in a rush. The circular park spreading in both directions from Trinity Methodist never again would be filled with the same enchanting colorful display.

Some of the particulars were changed that night, but the sentiment, the delight, and the neighborly feeling continue. The evening is one of joy, but the *cherished* moment occurs in the Tabernacle after the thousands of people who have been singing old standards and patriotic anthems supported by the very capable Vineyard Haven Band (which was organized in 1868) and enjoying arm-flailing audience participation continue to not just applaud, but *roar* their appreciation. Suddenly the lights are dimmed and all goes quiet.

On stage, a selected honoree, usually an elder, lights a candle set in a large paper lantern which is then, through the dark, carried down the center aisle to hang at the entrance arch. This marks the commencement of the "Grand Illumination," as the hundreds of colored lanterns encircling the structure blaze on at once and the cottagers bring their own charming porch displays to life. The delighted crowd spills out of the Tabernacle to saunter around the circular promenade, to view the houses in all their finery, and to ooh and aah at the fragile beauty of the few remaining antique silk lanterns brought home long ago by Island seafarers who enjoyed a brisk trade with the Orient during the age of sail.

Grand Illumination offers us many things—band music and song, the spotlighted beauty of Victorian architecture, and thousands of moonstruck lanterns gracing an enchanting nearly-150-year-old tradition. But the simplest, and yet greatest, gift of that lovely August night is the reminder of the power of a single light piercing the darkness.

19

Where Borogoves are Never Mimsy

'Twas brillig, and the slithy toves
Did gyre and gimble in the wabe;
All mimsy were the borogoves,
And the mome raths outgrabe.

Preceding the annual theatrical offering, the camp audience was treated to a dramatic and endearing recitation of Lewis Carroll's *Jabberwocky* by Helen Lamb ("Hellcat" to friends), 95-year-old queen of Camp Jabberwocky. Aging gracefully and creatively, this fine role model founded the camp for children and adults with disabilities in 1953 and it has run successfully and jubilantly on 99% volunteerism for all those years.

But! To the play! *The Labyrinth* is a story wherein young folk must travel to retrieve their baby brother who was snatched by The Fairy King himself! Thus unfolds the winding tale of the search through a complex series of sites (and beautiful sets) all within the Land of Fairies.

A huge cast comprising late August Jabberwocky campers and their counselors made up the list of actors, singers, musicians, dancers, and the chorus. What theatre provides the participant—always—is the opportunity to work in concert; to be part of a fleeting, but treasured co-creation; to don the mantle of another, gauging the fit of a new personality but for a moment; and to roam the realm of the imaginary—at once real, yet intangible.

A more engaging troupe of thespians is difficult to imagine: elated to be on stage, and anything but humble in accepting accolades . . . arms spread wide, the campers gather up the applause and uproarious response of the crowd and give it all a boisterous "hug." Actors are sometimes tortured souls . . . not this bunch . . . they know themselves all to be stars; moreover, they know *who* they are—and can produce entertaining theatre while not taking themselves seriously, a stunning achievement for any of us.

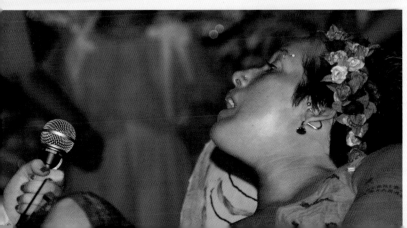

If your life is short on joy, hie thee to Camp Jabberwocky—and quickly, too—where life is lived with exquisite authenticity and the price of admission is the willingness to play!

20

Primal Power

At the Martha's Vineyard Agricultural Fair, which is lovingly and simply called "The Fair," the annual horse pull draws a large and dedicated crowd. The sheer beauty of the powerful horses, Norwegian Fjords and Belgians among them, is an arresting sight.

The horses work in concert with their drivers and "hookers" (the two standing to either side of the driver who controls the reins) hauling enormous weighted loads. Once the load is arranged and the team joins to the weight (which increases with every round), anticipation grips the men, the horses, and somehow, *especially* the audience. The air is electric. Then, all at once, the horses engage, and the sun highlights their muscles as they strain to haul the load. The ensuing clatter of the load chains and metal "evener" hitched to the load, the shouts of the men, and the snorts and pounding of hooves all melding together to move dead weight provide the embodiment of the curious calculation known as "horsepower."

For those who admire or crave a perhaps less complicated, but surely not a *simpler* life than what our contemporary one offers, watching these majestic horses, proudly—yes, *proudly*—straining at their bits and traces and pulling thousands of pounds of concrete, harkens us back and we are poised on a fulcrum of time and space.

The horses appear to understand the "showmanship" of their work; some even strut a bit approaching and leaving the ring. Though the competition between teams is sharp, sometimes a driver will drop out if he has a young horse who is tasting success, and the driver wants to keep it that way, bolstering the self-confidence of his team for the next competition. That kind of sensitivity to the nurturing of the animal as an individual and as part of a team is a fine gift. The deeper sense of communication between species is palpable.

That certain something about the horse pull—powerful and raw—draws us in and rivets us as we witness that visceral engagement—heightening the senses, centering the core.

21

Jellies and Preserves

Making jam and jelly is an age-old tradition. Beach plum and grape, apple, raspberry, peach, rosehip and blueberry—all manner of fruit, cultivated or wild, lend themselves beautifully to the process of coaxing out juice and pulp to be separated or blended, sweetened, and savored.

Gathering, washing, preparing, and rendering each batch is time-consuming and labor-intensive, requiring many hours—sometimes days—depending on the barometer. So why take on such a lengthy process when it's so easy to purchase commercial fruit products for a few dollars? And further, why do it the old-fashioned way which requires hours of boiling down the filtered juice to bring it to the density at which it will gel?

Home-made, in this case, *tastes* better and the lengthier process makes a jelly that tastes *best.* That could be reason enough—to provide the lucky recipient with the highest quality from one's kitchen. But taste is not the only reason.

When we partake in a tradition, we evoke the original sensory clues that surround the rituals, and for a short while, we are transported in time. Each sequential step is a ritual in itself and must precede or follow as always. Rituals and traditions reflect our values, so in their re-enactment our values are affirmed, and we are reminded of those who came before and who we came to be. The resulting sense of belonging to the group, the family, the community who passed down what is revered offers a sense of balance and grounding.

Making jelly the old-fashioned way, without modern-day short cuts, is a meditation. The sun is bright; the sky is clear; the voices of our grandmothers are on the wind.

22

Fair Winds of Change

Lively by day and sparkly by night, the Agricultural Fair was once confined to the narrow grounds at the Old Grange Hall, which separated the locally-run booths from the carnival amusement rides and games. We were all jammed in there and happy to be so.

The Hall was filled with beautiful flowers and succulent vegetables; the ten-foot sunflowers towered over displays of quilts, sweaters, pies, jellies, preserves, and artwork. Prize ribbons (including the treasured pale blue *Best in Show*) fluttered in the breeze—if August was kind. Out back, beyond the collection of ancient belching farm machinery, all manner of farm animals showed off their own array of ribbons, snorting, lowing, bleating, clucking, quacking, and neighing about the end-of-summer doings.

When the fair was moved to the sprawling acres of the new Ag Hall, the intermittent local booths were widely spaced from each other as well as from the carnival games and rides. Though the exhibits increased, their arrangement seemed sparse and sad in the immensity of the new Hall. The locals grumbled as the coziness of the Grange grounds was lost.

But the visionaries' predictions were quickly realized. As a community, we grew into the space. With a fourth day of events added and an increasing number and variety of local booths and carnie rides in place, everyone is now snugged up next to each other and the fair, having lost none of its charm, is cozy once more.

What's traditional at the fair makes it comfortable; what's new keeps it fresh. Those with gyroscopes in their bellies still throw caution to the wind to spin backwards and upside-down. Games of chance still satisfy our desire to beat the odds. We still delight in our neighbors' creations in the kitchen, studio, and garden. We can still do all these things while sporting temporary tattoos at the new piggy races.

After summer-long anticipation, fair breezes blow. Of the broad variety of experiences offered by the annual fair, the sweetest is the opportunity, in a mood of nonchalance, to see people who've been too busy *making* a summer living to *make* time to sit and chat. The ways the fair changed are completely overshadowed by its most important aspect—playfully sharing a little bit of summer with family and friends.

23

Summer's Lullaby

The end of summer is a sequence of scheduling "lasts" and recalling "firsts." When summer wanes, vacationers make time for the last sail, the last cocktail party or cookout, the last ride on the Flying Horses, the last view of the cliffs, the last kiss from a summer sweetheart, the last leap off the "big bridge," the last romp around the Ocean Park bandstand, the last fishing trip, the last lobster dinner, the last search for the perfect souvenir, the last beach day, and of course, the last swim, no matter what the weather.

When the fair grounds have emptied and the amusement rides have been folded onto their trucks; when the paper lanterns are once more stored away; when the twinkle, sizzle, and thunder of the Oak Bluffs fireworks have worked their magic, the last goodbyes are said and the season's events are packaged in memory to be opened as needed when school and work intrude once more.

Winter will unfurl the sensory-laden images of summer: that first shout of welcome on the long-awaited return, the season's first shriek as the waves still holding a little bit of February reach the belly button, napping on the beach with sandy toes and salt-crusted hair, the baby's first taste of sun-baked seaweed, community sing at the Tabernacle, the pungent burst of a deep-fried clam belly, coming about in a twenty-knot wind, blessings counted at a summer worship, catching the first bluefish on a dancing sea, the first glimpse of "Seal Island" off Muskeget Shoals, the deep note of the fog horn on a cool and misty night.

But on the day of farewell to the sweet season, tucked in along with the clothing and toys and the paraphernalia of vacation already crammed into the car, is the sea glass and rock collection and the 'great find' not quite petrified enough to prevent the eventual surprise of the potent scent of its lingering decay.

Before that ferry ride the vacationer savors that last renewing, soul-deep, and dreamless sleep peculiar to islands and all through the night, the crickets sing summer's lullaby.

24

Shore and Shoals

When I was a kid in Oak Bluffs, every autumn night during the month-long annual fishing derby we rode our bikes to town to watch the weighing in of huge striped bass. A long line of hopefuls wound out the door, each fisherman holding his largest fish of the day by the gill slit. Mr. Hartman, the weigh master, flipped the big fish onto the scale pan, the needle swung, and the weight was pronounced. As Helen Scarborough entered the information in her ledger, the crowd moaned or whooped according to their loyalties to the record holder. Everyone murmured and someone would always say, "Boy, that's a nice fish."

It was glorious—it was the *only* show in town. Except for two grocery stores, the post office, a hardware store, the coffee shop, and a clothing store, everything else had been boarded up since Labor Day, the official end of summer when the tourists left and a crispness snapped the air right on schedule. At night, the only other lights downtown were from the bar.

Anyone at the weigh-in station (a bare storefront with a cement floor with a drain, a water source and hose, the scales, and the competition boards) foolish enough to ask what kind of tackle or bait was used was told a fish story. If marinated pork rinds had been used, surely the fisherman would say "Eel." No matter if the catch site was off Dogfish Bar, Middle Ground, East Beach, Devil's Bridge, or the Wharf, all answers to "Where'd you catch that fish?" were, "Long Beach."

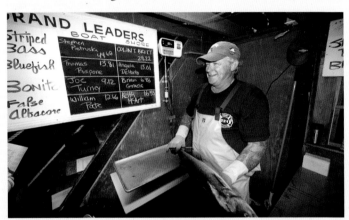

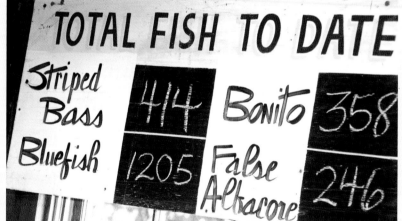

The bass derby is now incorporated as a non-profit and entitled The Martha's Vineyard Striped Bass and Bluefish Derby, Inc., and not only bass, but categories of blues, bonito, and false albacore grace the boards. More women make the boards now—and juniors, too. Sponsorship and prizes have increased. And a substantial annual scholarship is provided for local high school seniors. Personnel, still jovial, are more numerous; the scale is digital, the "ledger" computerized. Environmental changes, factory ships scooping up bait fish, an increasing seal population, and unfavorable weather all have impact.

What hasn't changed is the camaraderie, the good friendships made, the love of bouncing on the waves or standing watch on the shore with lines in the water. Eels, squid, pork rinds, rubber and sparkly lures, all sorts of bait still snag fish, though fishermen sometimes need to reel in faster than the chasing seals can swim. Politics between fishermen still bubble under the surface or erupt sometimes. The weigh-in station is now on the dock in Edgartown, the fillet master on a floating dock nearby deftly boning and skinning fish for a program for Island elders. The exuberance of competition, the joy of the outdoors and living life fully in it—bundled up and beak to the wind—still affords its own deep-seated and unequalled pleasures. The sense of fishing hard and enjoying the derby no matter what the challenges of weather and circumstance still ignite the passion of participating in something very deeply "Vineyard." Fishermen continue to tell their own truths and all fish are caught at Long Beach, which is still in California.

25

Balance on the Half Shell

The Island's greatest natural resource for family or commercial fishermen has always been pristine waters. Getting a mess of clams or quahaugs, oysters, or scallops is well-suited to the independent nature of Islanders. Time spent "on the pond," oddly enough, inspires a joyous feeling of being *beyond* the realm of time.

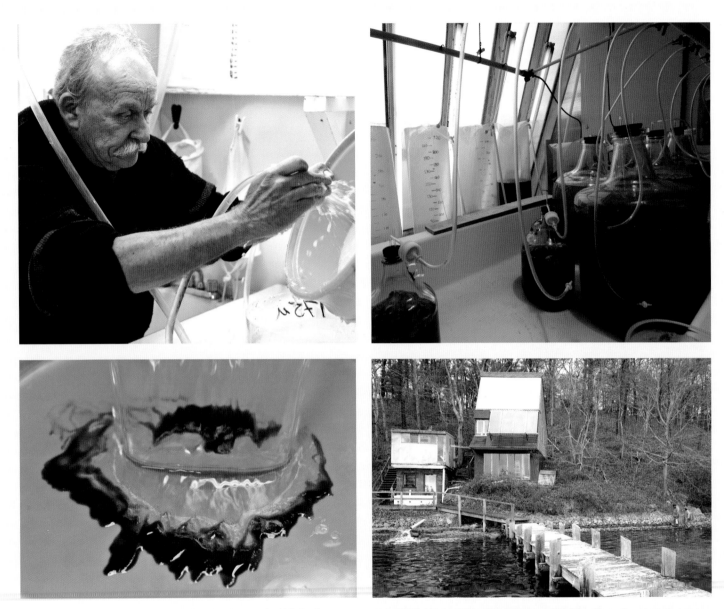

Well-thought out attempts to create shellfish farms were made here in the 1940s and 1960s. But, having been horn-swoggled a time or two by "opportunities," local people feared the loss of the availability of the ponds as sources of livelihood, thereby mistaking an inherently beneficial *legitimate* opportunity for a scenario to undermine home rule. Their resulting political actions postponed hatchery and shellfish farming for a good long time.

The derailment of those potentially successful endeavors—which might well have sustained their independence—occurred at a time when the hearty seeds of tourism began to sprout as never before, and the Island became increasingly dependent on the summer trade.

The Martha's Vineyard Shellfish Group, a public amalgamation of the shellfish departments of the Island's towns with biologist Rick Karney at the helm, began its highly successful hatchery in the mid-70s spawning millions of baby quahaugs, scallops, and oysters to seed and augment the natural production in our shallow salt water ponds and bays. Through constant research, enormous strides have been made and we are now well informed of the opportunities of shellfisheries. MVSG's grant-funded training program on oyster farming was so successful that more than a dozen private oyster growers currently farm Katama and Menemsha Ponds.

Relying on tourism as a solo industry has taken a great toll, and so—enter the oyster. Aside from being a delightful morsel to prepare in a stew or slurp up raw, this crinkly-shelled mollusk is an environmental maintenance mechanism—filtering out impurities and generally "cleaning house" for all its neighbors. Proof that the oyster's residency predates human habitation on the Island suggests other solutions may be nestled right where Mother Nature intended.

The shellfishing industry offers expansion and renewal for local species and the oyster boasts a stable global market. Balancing tourism once more with a sustainable year-round industry could profoundly affect the lives of the Island's children, providing a revitalized source of independence. We are well aware of the boundless gifts of a life lived intimately with Nature—and nothing quite compares with a day on the pond.

26

Sustainability

The expansion of summer into the "shoulder seasons," the increase in populations in all seasons, and the absorption of so much formerly wild, undeveloped land into building lots, large and small, have collectively altered the landscape and the condition of resources above and below the ground, have minimized accessibility of people and animals, and thus, have impacted our way of life.

The popularization of paradise is an old theme, and so is the tension it spawns. Those concerned with the interrelationship of all things (more poignant here as our island is finite) are almost invariably at odds with those who forget to consider that short-term actions can have long-term impact.

Therein lies the challenge: how to preserve and sustain that which is sacred, often fragile, in a fast-paced consumer society. Efforts to strike a balance between old and new have often lagged just far enough behind the pace of change to prevent valued things from being lost forever.

The Vineyard has her own inner life and she taps the wellspring of renewal from deep within, drawing up that which revitalizes our senses and more, gentling the psyche, and connecting us with an unnamable essence far beyond the mundane.

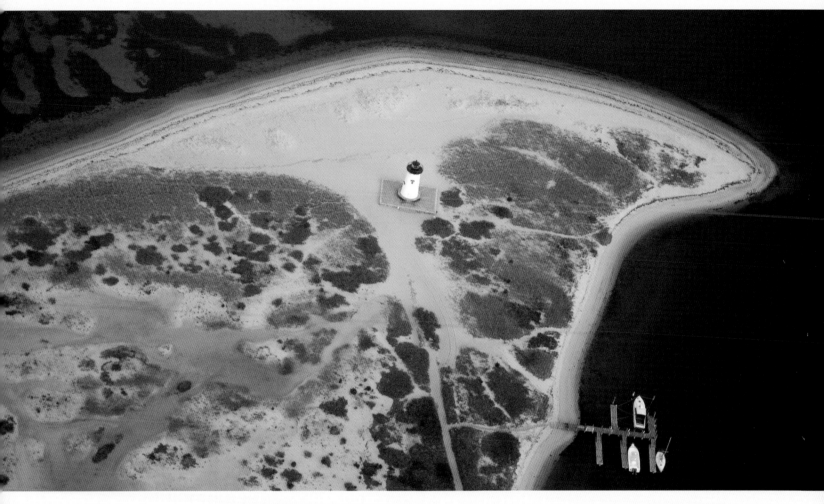

Counterpoint to the pursuit of the resolution of multi-layered social, economic, and environmental issues, is the truly daunting concept that recent rapid growth threatens the very nature of that enchanting and soul-soothing "something" that makes Martha's Vineyard unique.

Islanders, from the beginning, have practiced a mindful stewardship. Drawing deeply on that tradition of participation and respectful exchange, we can regain a balance, insuring that renewal is a fact of life honoring the unspoken promise we and this once-pristine Island make to each other—and thus, to those who will follow.

27

Now and Zen

The inhabitants keep the island "anchored at sea," out of time and not in sync with the ever-increasing pace of society's evolution away from our spiritual center. While others may encourage a frenzied pace, there are those here who take a while to dance to the rhythm, steadfastly maintaining the familiar backbeat, guided by the seasons. They're the ones who've made a practice of staring for long periods out to sea. We rely on them to feel that pulse, the thrum beneath the sand. They're the ones who keep us real.